Great White Sharks

By Moira Rose Donohue

Children's Press®

An Imprint of Scholastic Inc.

Content Consultant
Becky Ellsworth
Curator, Shores Region
Columbus Zoo and Aquarium

Library of Congress Cataloging-in-Publication Data
Names: Donohue, Moira Rose, author.
Title: Great white sharks/by Moira Rose Donohue.
Description: New York, NY: Children's Press, an Imprint of Scholastic Inc., 2018. |
Series: Nature's children | Includes index.
Identifiers: LCCN 2017041061| ISBN 9780531234839 (library binding) | ISBN 9780531245132 (pbk.)
Subjects: LCSH: White shark—Juvenile literature.
Classification: LCC QL638.95.L3 D66 2018 | DDC 597.3/3—dc23
LC record available at https://lccn.loc.gov/2017041061

Design by Anna Tunick Tabachnik

Creative Direction: Judith Christ-Lafond for Scholastic

Produced by Spooky Cheetah Press

Printed in China 62

SCHOLASTIC, CHILDREN'S PRESS, NATURE'S CHILDREN™, and associated logos
are trademarks and/or registered trademarks of Scholastic Inc.

2 3 4 5 6 7 8 9 10 R 27 26 25 24 23 22 21 20 19 18

Scholastic Inc., 557 Broadway, New York, NY 10012.

Photos ©: cover: Chris and Monique Fallows/Minden Pictures; 1: Reinhard Dirscherl/Getty Images; 4 leaf silo and throughout: stockgraphicdesigns.com; 5 child silo: All-Silhouettes.com; 5 bottom: Ken Kiefer 2/Getty Images; 6 shark silo and throughout: daulon/Shutterstock; 7: Alessandro De Maddalena/Shutterstock; 8-9: Rainer Schimpf/Barcroft Animals/Barcroft Media/ Getty Images; 11 bottom: Walter Geiersperger/Getty Images; 11 top: Reinhard Dirscherl/Getty Images; 12-13: Denis Scott/Getty Images; 15: Keren Su/Getty Images; 16-17: Jennifer Hayes/Getty Images; 18-19: USO/iStockphoto; 20-21 main: Chris & Monique Fallows/Nature Picture Library/Getty Images; 20 inset: Clouds Hill Imaging Ltd./Getty Images; 23: Pascal Kobeh/NPL/Minden Pictures; 24 top left: Shinji Kusano/Nature Production/Minden Pictures; 24 top right: Joost van Uffelen/Getty Images; 24 bottom left: Rodrigo Friscione/Getty Images; 24 bottom right: Awashima Marine Park/Getty Images; 26-27: Anthony Pierce/ Alamy Images; 28-29: Mike Parry/Minden Pictures; 31 main: The Granger Collection; 31 background: Greg and Jan Ritchie/ Shutterstock; 32-33: by wildestanimal/Getty Images; 34-35: Steve Woods Photography/Getty Images; 37: Doug Perrine/Getty Images; 38-39: Auscape/UIG/Getty Images; 40-41: Reinhard Dirscherl/ullstein bild/Getty Images; 42 bottom: Joel Sartore/ National Geographic Creative; 42 center: Irochka_T/iStockphoto; 42 top: Paulo Oliveira/Alamy Images; 43 center: Andrew Seale/WaterFrame/age fotostock; 43 top left: Nataliya Taratunina/Shutterstock; 43 top right: BlueOrange Studio/123RF; 43 bottom: Reinhard Dirscherl/Getty Images.

Maps by Jim McMahon.

Table of Contents

Fact File **4**

CHAPTER 1   **King Fish** **6**
     A Huge Habitat 9
     Built to Hunt 10
     Fearsome Jaws 13

CHAPTER 2   **Ocean Prowler** **14**
     Out of the Blue 17
     Shark Sense 18
     Superfast 21

CHAPTER 3   **Born to Rule** **22**
     A Long Wait 25
     Born Swimming 26
     School of One 29

CHAPTER 4   **Fishy Family** **30**
     New Ancestors 33
     My Cousin Ray 34

CHAPTER 5   **The Ocean Without Sharks** **36**
     Man vs. Shark 39
     Shark Tank 40

Great White Shark Family Tree **42**
Words to Know **44**
Find Out More **46**
Facts for Now **46**
Index **47**
About the Author **48**

Fact File: Great White Sharks

World Distribution

Mainly temperate oceans and coastal areas around the world

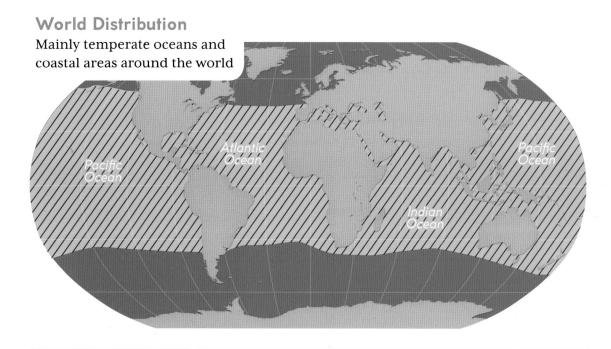

Pacific Ocean

Atlantic Ocean

Pacific Ocean

Indian Ocean

Population Status
Vulnerable

Habitats
Open ocean and coastal areas around the world

Habits
Live mostly in temperate waters

Diet
Mainly marine mammals like seals and sea lions; sometimes fish

Distinctive Features
streamlined, torpedo-shaped bodies with huge projecting jaws; rows of sharp, serrated teeth

Fast Fact
Great whites can survive for several weeks without eating.

Average Length

16 ft.
(4.9 m)

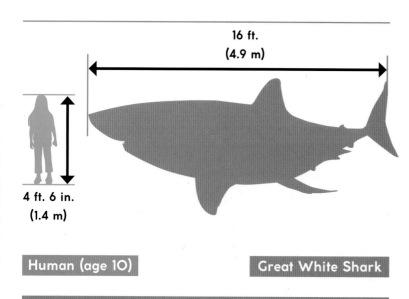

4 ft. 6 in.
(1.4 m)

Human (age 10)

Great White Shark

Taxonomy

CLASS
Chondrichthyes
(fish)

ORDER
Lamniformes
(mackerel sharks)

FAMILY
Lamnidae
(mako, salmon shark,
porbeagle, great white)

GENUS
Carcharodon
(great white and
extinct ancestors only)

SPECIES
carcharias
(great white)

COMMON NAMES
great white shark,
white shark, white
pointer

◀ As shown here, a
great white's eye looks
dull and black, but it is
actually blue.

CHAPTER 1

King Fish

It's quiet in the Pacific Ocean. The late-afternoon sun sparkles across the surface of the water. A sea lion glides near its home off the coast of San Francisco, California. In a flash, the surface of the ocean is broken by a huge mouth. Chomp! The sharp teeth of a great white shark bite down on the sea lion.

Great white sharks live in all of Earth's oceans. They can swim thousands of miles in a year. The average great white shark weighs between 2,500 and 5,000 pounds (1,134 and 2,268 kilograms). In the ocean, it is an apex **predator**. That means this fish is at the top of the marine food chain.

So how can its **population** be shrinking? Great whites may rule the water, but humans have put them at risk. Fishing has killed off millions of sharks, including the great white. Today, this important fish is considered **vulnerable**, and may become **extinct**.

▶ A great white flips through the air as it snatches a seal.

Fast Fact
A great white
can smell a colony
of seals 2 mi.
(3.2 km) away.

A Huge Habitat

Great white sharks are pelagic. That means they swim in open water all around the world. In such a large habitat, scientists often have trouble finding and studying them.

Great whites can be found gliding near coasts, too. They have at least three favorite spots. At certain times, these sharks cluster near the sandy shores of Kangaroo Island, Australia. They also hang out at Seal Island off the coast of South Africa. And in fall, they are often spotted around the rocky coast of the Farallon Islands, 30 miles (48.3 kilometers) from San Francisco, California. All three places have something in common. They are nurseries for baby seals and sea lions—the great white's favorite food.

Parts of Earth's oceans are chilly. But these sharks don't mind. They can adapt because, unlike other fish, they have an internal thermometer. Great whites can raise their body temperature. This helps them digest food in cold water. It also gives them a burst of energy to snatch a tasty snack.

◀ A great white hunts
in the waters near Seal
Island in South Africa.

Built to Hunt

The great white is perfectly designed for its role as the ocean's top predator. Though it may not be the biggest fish in the sea, this shark is still pretty huge! The average great white is 12 to 16 feet (3.7 to 4.9 meters) long. That's about as long as a minivan. Some grow to 21 ft. (6.4 m) or more!

Great white sharks are shaped like torpedoes, so they cut through the water. Their most recognizable features are probably their fins and giant tooth-filled jaws.

These creatures need oxygen, just as we humans do. But they don't breathe air. They breathe water. Sharks swim with their mouths open. Water flows in. Then it flows out through their gills, which are slits on their sides. The shark's body absorbs oxygen from the water as it passes over the gills. If a great white shark stops swimming, it won't be able to breathe.

Caudal (or Tail) Fin

gives the shark its explosive burst of speed.

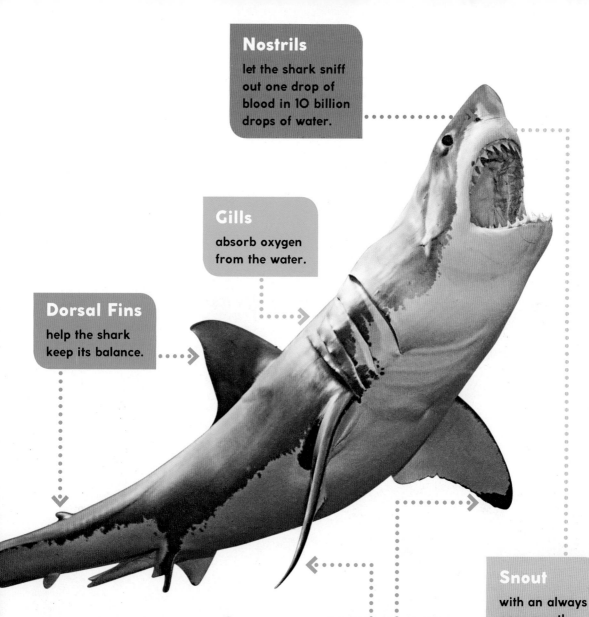

Nostrils
let the shark sniff out one drop of blood in 10 billion drops of water.

Gills
absorb oxygen from the water.

Dorsal Fins
help the shark keep its balance.

Snout
with an always open mouth allows water to flow in as the shark swims.

Teeth
have serrated edges that cut like a knife.

Pectoral Fins
help the shark steer through the water.

Fearsome Jaws

Humans' jaws are hinged and attached to our skulls, so they can open only so far. The great white shark's jaw isn't **fused** to its skull. When it sees a large animal, it lifts its snout high and drops its lower jaw. Then the shark thrusts its entire jaw forward. Crunch! No meal is too big for this toothy predator.

The great white shark's genus name, *Carcharodon*, comes from the Greek words for "sharp or jagged" and "tooth." Its teeth are triangular, and each is **serrated**. The great white has 26 top teeth and 24 bottom teeth in the front of its mouth. Rows of hundreds of new teeth are hidden right behind them. That's because a great white loses teeth at almost every meal. When that happens, a tooth in the next row moves forward to fill the gap. This shark's teeth are only for biting. The great white can't chew its food. Instead, it bites off large chunks and swallows them whole.

◀ A great white can use up thousands of teeth during its lifetime.

CHAPTER 2

Ocean Prowler

When most people think of a great white on the hunt, they picture a menacing giant gliding silently through the water. But a great white shark can actually leap completely out of the water when it spies something to eat. The shark bites down once on its **prey**. Then it often lets go. The shark may be waiting for the animal to die before eating it. Or it may not like the taste.

When you're at the top of the food chain, you can eat anything you want. Great whites chow down on fish, squid, dolphins, and even parts of dead whales. They usually target young, old, or sick animals. Sometimes they catch a sea turtle, pelican, penguin, or sea otter.

Though great whites can—and do—eat just about anything, these sharks have a favorite food: **pinnipeds**, like walruses, seals, and sea lions. These animals have a lot of body fat, some of which the shark stores in its liver. That helps the shark survive when food is hard to find.

▶ When a shark leaps out of the water it is called breaching.

Out of the Blue

The great white shark is clever. It has to be to hunt intelligent animals like sea lions. This cunning killer often hunts by ambush. It lurks underneath its prey. Sometimes it follows just behind, shadowing the animal. Then, with two flicks of its rear fin, the shark explodes forward and grabs a meal.

The great white also surprises its prey by using **camouflage**. The shark's colors hide this fish from animals that it wants to eat. Despite its name, the great white is only white on its belly. Its back is gray or dark brown. From underneath, the shark blends in with the sunlit water. From above, it seems to be part of the darker ocean floor.

◀ This shark can see the sea lion, but the sea lion doesn't know it's being followed.

Shark Sense

Sharks have the same five senses that humans do. But a shark's senses are heightened for life in the deep blue sea.

Sharks have very good vision, even in low light. And their eyes have a unique form of protection. Great whites don't have eyelids that close. These sharks roll their eyes back into their sockets to keep them from getting injured.

The great white also has excellent hearing and a keen sense of smell. And, like other fish, the great white has a **lateral** line along each side of its body that allows it to feel **vibrations** in the water.

In addition to these "super" senses, sharks also have a sixth sense: ampullae of Lorenzini. These jelly-filled pores on a shark's snout detect electrical currents given off by Earth's magnetic field—like a built-in compass to navigate underwater.

▶ The great white has a distinct color separation between its back and underbelly.

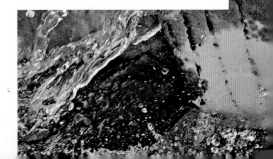

▲ magnified detail
of denticles

Superfast

The great white is fast. It can swim 25 miles per hour (40.1 kilometers per hour) or more as it ambushes its prey.

One reason this giant fish can race so fast is that its body is super flexible. It has no bones! The great white's skeleton is made up of **cartilage**, like your outer ears.

But another secret to the great white's speed is its skin. If you run your hand over the skin of a dolphin, it feels like a boiled egg. But if you could get close enough to run your hand over the body of a great white, you might get scraped. That's because the great white is covered in scales called **denticles**. They look like tiny, pointy teeth. These scales lower the **resistance** that slows an object down as it glides through water or air. Olympic swimmers have taken a lesson from these sharks. Many have had swimsuits made out of a rough fabric like this shark's skin.

◀ Because it has no bones, the great white is as flexible as rubber.

CHAPTER 3

Born to Rule

Great whites are always on the move.

But in late spring and summer, lots of male great whites from the North American coast hang around in one area in the Pacific Ocean. It's about halfway between San Francisco, California, and the Hawaiian Islands.

There is no land nearby. Experts are not sure, but they think this might be a mating area. They have nicknamed it the "White Shark Café."

The great white shark can live to be 60 years old or older. It doesn't mate until it is at least 10 years old. Over and over, the mature males dive down to the bright blue depths. Females float into the area from time to time. But they don't stay long—just long enough to mate. Pregnant females often have bite marks on their backs. The male bites down on the female's back to hold on to it.

▶ The bite marks on this female tell us she has mated several times.

Sea Horse

▶ A male sea horse can give birth and then be pregnant again in the same day!

Blue Shark

▶ This shark can have a litter of up to 100 pups or more!

Mola Fish

▶ A mola fish can release 300 million eggs over one season.

Frilled Shark

▶ This shark's pregancy can last three and a half years.

A Long Wait

Mammals, such as people and dogs, give birth to live babies. Most fish lay eggs—often thousands of them. But not the great white shark. Her eggs hatch inside her body, and her babies, called pups, are born live.

The female great white has a litter about every two years. Most females have about 12 eggs in a litter. Each egg develops within a special pouch inside the female. Experts think it takes 12 to 18 months for the eggs to mature and hatch. That's a long time to wait!

On average, only five shark pups are actually born. Some of them die before they hatch. And scientists think that the first to hatch may eat its brother and sister sharks while still inside their mother.

Some types of sharks go to a shallow, safe place to give birth. But scientists have not been able to watch great white pups being born. They think some great whites go to warm waters off the coast of Mexico to have their babies.

◀ All these creatures
are fish, like the great
white shark. They
all have fascinating
reproduction stories!

Born Swimming

Baby great whites are about 4 ft. (1.2 m) long and weigh about 40 lb. (18.1 kg) when they are born. That's about the size of an average human kindergartner. Great white shark pups grow about a foot a year. By the time they are 10 years old, they are fully grown.

Many animal babies need their mothers to teach them how to hunt or swim. But not these pups. They are born swimming. And they already know how to hunt. As soon as they are born, they start grabbing nearby fish. Their mothers just swim away.

These powerful predators are actually shy and cautious. They circle around new things, slowly getting closer and closer. But they are also curious. Usually their curiosity wins out. That's when they bite. They are trying to taste-test what they have found.

▶ This pup was in an aquarium for just over six months—the longest a great white ever survived in captivity.

School of One

Great whites don't stay together as families. And they don't travel in schools, like other fish. They are generally loners. In fact, sometimes a male will slap its tail out of the water to warn a nearby shark to move on.

But one shark expert made an interesting discovery. He found a group of great whites swimming together without being aggressive. As the diver continued to watch, two sharks swam closer to him. And they swam together, side by side, like **synchronized** swimmers.

The expert noticed that the sharks had almost identical markings on their fins. That's unusual. In fact, each great white shark has different markings on its large dorsal fin—a unique *fin*-gerprint. Maybe these sharks were brothers. Or maybe sharks aren't the loners scientists thought they were.

◀ Every great white looks different, and each one has its own personality.

CHAPTER 4

Fishy Family

Sharks have been around for over 400 million years. Today there are more than 400 **species**. Some sharks are small. The dwarf lantern shark is no longer than a pencil. The biggest is the spotted whale shark. It can grow up to 32.8 ft. (9.9 m) long. This gentle giant eats only tiny plants and animals.

Scientists used to think that the great white was related to the ancient shark called megalodon. It lived more than 15 million years ago and is now extinct.

Megalodon was a giant fish. Its tooth was the size of a grown man's hand. Several children could stand in its open jaws. It was probably 40 to 50 ft. (12.2 to 15.2 m) long. That's as long as a school bus. And it weighed more than five elephants put together!

Like the great white of today, it had no bones. The only **fossils** it left behind are its teeth.

▶ This megalodon's reconstructed jaw is about 30 times as big as a great white's jaw.

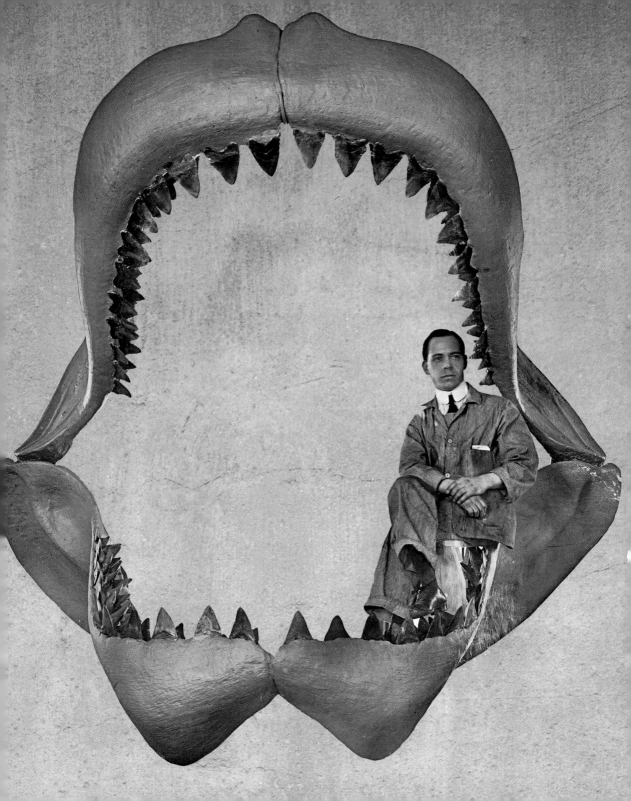

New Ancestors

Sometimes people discover that they have relatives they didn't know about. That happened to the great white. Recently scientists found evidence that it wasn't directly related to the megalodon.

A fossil collector discovered a set of jaws in Peru, South America. Experts who studied the jaws found that they belonged to a shark no one had seen before. They named it the Hubbell shark, after the man who found the fossil.

The Hubbell shark's teeth are a cross between the mako shark's choppers and the great white's. Megalodon had similar teeth—and a powerful bite—but it's not related to the great white after all. The scientists decided that the Hubbell shark was the **ancestor** of both the great white and the mako shark.

The shortfin mako is the fastest shark in the ocean. It travels at more than 20 mph (32.2 kph) and can have speed bursts of up to 45 mph (72.4 kph).

◄ The mako shark has between 11 and 13 rows of teeth.

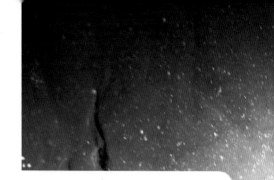

My Cousin Ray

Rays and skates are flat fish that are related to great white sharks. Like their massive cousins, these fish have no bones. They look like sharks that have been run over by a truck! Because they are flat, they often rest on the ocean floor. Many blend into the sand.

There are more than 500 types of rays. Some, like the stingray, have venomous spines at the base of their tails. Others, like the electric ray, can give off a charge of electricity.

The largest ray of all is the manta ray. It can grow to about 23 ft. (7 m) across. Like the great white, the manta ray is dark on its back and white underneath. This big fish is harmless to humans.

▶ Like the great white's dorsal fin, each manta ray's underside has unique markings.

CHAPTER 5

The Ocean Without Sharks

Great whites have a bad reputation.

Many people think these giants are man-eaters. But great whites don't hunt humans for food.

Great white sharks bite things when they are curious. They probably bite people just to see if they are food. And after biting a person, the shark usually spits him or her out. We don't taste good to them! A great white shark bite is dangerous. But almost everyone who is bitten survives.

Because many people are afraid of sharks, they are not interested in protecting them. But our oceans need protection. And that means sharks do, too! The ocean is an **ecosystem**. It's a community of different kinds of plants and animals that need each other. The great white shark helps the community stay in balance by preventing certain animal populations, like sea lions, from getting too large.

▶ To a shark, a person on a surfboard can look like a seal—tasty prey.

Man vs. Shark

Sadly, humans kill about 100 million sharks every year. Why? In some parts of the world, they are needed for food. But most shark deaths are unnecessary.

Some people hunt and kill sharks just for their teeth and their fins. Shark fins are used to make an expensive luxury food—shark fin soup. But sharks can't live without their fins.

Shark parts are also sometimes used in traditional medicines. But scientists have proven that there is no real medical value to these so-called cures.

Some sharks are killed accidentally. They are often trapped in large nets that are meant to catch other types of fish. Also, water **pollution** harms all the animals of the ocean, including the great white shark.

The great white doesn't have a lot of pups at a time. And it takes a long time for them to be born. So when these animals die, there aren't enough sharks being born to replace them. That's why the great white is in trouble.

◀ Fishing nets can be deadly for sharks, like the one trapped here.

Shark Tank

How can we help? First, we need to learn as much as we can about sharks. But that's hard. Traditionally, great whites have not been able to survive in **captivity**. Scientists are just beginning to understand how humans can care for them in tanks. In the meantime, scientists have to study great white sharks in the ocean.

Some brave experts dive in the ocean in shark-proof cages to watch these animals in the wild. Others sail the oceans to find them. Then they insert a special tag into the shark's dorsal fin. It doesn't hurt the shark, and it allows scientists to track the shark's movements. That teaches the researchers about behavior and travel patterns.

Governments can help, too. They can limit shark killing. And they can set up protected areas for sharks.

You have already helped just by learning about these amazing creatures. You can help spread the word about how important these powerful predators are to a healthy ocean—and how important it is to protect them.

▶ Scientists use food to lure sharks close to the cage.

Fast Fact
In South Africa, tourists can watch sharks from diving cages.

Great White Shark Family Tree

Great whites are a type of shark. Like all sharks, they are fish. Fish are cold-blooded animals that live in water and have scales, fins, and gills. Fish comprise more than 28,000 species. They all share a common ancestor that lived 360 million years ago. This diagram shows how sharks are related to some other fish. The closer together two animals are on the tree, the more similar they are.

Chimæras
deep-sea fish with soft bodies, pointed snouts, and skeletons made of cartilage

Bony Fish
fish with fins for swimming and skeletons made of bone

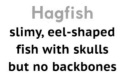

Hagfish
slimy, eel-shaped fish with skulls but no backbones

Ancestor of all Fish

Note: Sizes of animals are not to scale.

Skates

**fish with flat,
diamond-shaped
bodies, fleshy
tails, and fins
on their backs**

Rays

**fish with flat,
diamond-shaped
bodies, whiplike
tails, and no
back fins**

Sawfish

**flat-bodied fish
with long, narrow
snouts covered
in teeth**

Great White Sharks

**fish with cartilage
skeletons, strong jaws,
and sandpapery skin**

Words to Know

A .... **adapt** *(a-DAPT)* to change because you are in a different situation

ancestor *(ANN-ses-tur)* a family member who lived long ago

C .... **camouflage** *(KAM-uh-flahzh)* a way of hiding by using coloring, pattern, or shape to blend into one's surroundings

captivity *(kap-TIV-i-tee)* the condition of living in the care of people

cartilage *(KAHR-tuh-lij)* a strong, elastic tissue like the one that forms the outer ear and nose of humans and mammals and lines the bones at the joints

D .... **denticles** *(DEN-tik-uhls)* small teeth or toothlike projections

E .... **ecosystem** *(EE-koh-sis-tuhm)* all the living things in a place and their relation to their environment

extinct *(ik-STINGKT)* no longer found alive

F .... **fossils** *(FAH-suhls)* bones, shells, or other traces of an animal or plant from millions of years ago, preserved as rock

fused *(FYOOZD)* joined or grown together

H .... **habitat** *(HAB-i-tat)* the place where an animal or plant is usually found

L .... **lateral** *(LAT-ur-uhl)* on, at, from, or to the side

M .... **mammals** *(MAM-uhlz)* warm-blooded animals that have hair or fur and usually give birth to live babies; female mammals produce milk to feed their young

N.......... **nurseries** *(NUR-sur-eez)* where baby animals sleep

P.......... **pelagic** *(puh-LAJ-ik)* living in the open sea

pinnipeds *(PIH-neh-peds)* marine mammals in the seal or walrus family with four flippers

pollution *(puh-LOO-shuhn)* harmful materials that damage or contaminate the air, water, and soil, such as chemicals, gasoline exhaust, industrial waste, and excessive noise and light

population *(pahp-yuh-LAY-shuhn)* all members of a species living in a certain place

predator *(PRED-uh-tuhr)* an animal that lives by hunting other animals for food

prey *(PRAY)* an animal that is hunted by another animal for food

R.......... **resistance** *(ri-ZIS-tuhns)* a force that opposes the motion of an object

S.......... **serrated** *(SER-ay-tid)* having a blade like that of a saw

species *(SPEE-sheez)* one of the groups into which animals and plants are divided; members of the same species can mate and have offspring

synchronized *(SING-kruh-nized)* happening at the same time

V.......... **vibrations** *(vye-BRAY-shuhnz)* small, rapid movements back and forth or from side to side

vulnerable *(VUHL-nur-uh-buhl)* facing threats and likely to become endangered

Find Out More

BOOKS

- Arlon, Penelope. *Discover More: Sharks*. New York: Scholastic, 2013.
- Cerullo, Mary M. *The Truth about Great White Sharks*. San Francisco: Chronicle Books, 2000.
- Musgrave, Ruth A., with David Doubilet and Jennifer Hayes. *National Geographic Kids: Everything Sharks*. Washington, D.C.: National Geographic Society, 2011.

WEB PAGES

- www.floridamuseum.ufl.edu/fish/discover/species-profiles/carcharodon-carcharias

  The Florida Museum of Natural History provides one of the most authoritative Web sites on great white sharks.

- www.ocean.si.edu/great-white-shark

  This Smithsonian Institution site offers facts, photos, and more.

- www.kids.nationalgeographic.com/animals/great-white-shark/#great-whiteshark-swimming-blue.jpg

  The *National Geographic Kids* Web site offers fascinating—and funny—facts about the ocean's top predator.

Facts for Now

Visit this Scholastic Web site for more information on great white sharks: **www.factsfornow.scholastic.com** Enter the keywords Great White Sharks

Index

A

ampullae of Lorenzini....................18

Australia...9

B

bites........6, *7*, 13, 14, 22, *23*, 26, 33, 36

blue shark...............................24, *24*

breathing.................................10, 11

C

captivity............................26, *27*, 40

cartilage.......................................21

coasts............................6, 9, 22, 25

D

denticles................................ *20*, 21

dorsal fin.................11, *11*, 29, 34, 40

dwarf lantern shark......................30

E

ecosystem....................................36

extinction................................6, 30

F

fins............10, 11, *11*, 17, 29, 34, 39, 40

fossils................................30, *31*, 33

frilled shark............................24, *24*

G

gills.....................................10, 11, *11*

H

Hubbell shark..............................33

hunting techniques....6, *7*, *8*, 9, 13, 14, *15*, *16*, 17, *20*, 21, 26, 34, 36

J

jaws.....................10, *12*, 13, 30, *31*, 33

L

lateral line....................................18

lifespan..22

M

mako...*32*, 33

markings...........................29, 34, *35*

mating...22

megalodon....................30, *31*, 33

Mexico...25

mola fish..............................24, *24*

P

pelagic...9

predator...................6, 10, 13, 26, 40

prey.....................*6*, 7, *8*, 9, 14, *15*, *16*, 17, 36, 21, *37*

Index *(continued)*

pups 24, 25, 26, *27*, 39

R

rays 34, *35*

reproduction 22, 25

S

San Francisco.......................... 6, 9, 22

sea horse 24, *24*

senses.................................... 9, 11, 18

shark fin soup............................. 39

size 6, 10, 26, 30, 33

skates 34

skin *20*, 21

South Africa......................... *8*, 9, 41

speed................................. 10, 21, 33

status... 6

T

teeth........ 6, 10, 11, *11*, *12*, 13, *28*, 30, *31*, 33, 39

threats............................ 6, 36, *38*, 39

tracking....................................... 40

traditional medicines................... 39

V

vibrations 18

W

whale shark 30, 33

"White Shark Café" 22

About the Author

Moira Rose Donohue, a former attorney, is an animal lover and has written over 25 books for children, including many about animals. She lives with her two dogs in northern Virginia and St. Petersburg, Florida.